ANIMAL RECORD BREAKERS

AFRICAN ELEPHANT

THE LARGEST LAND MAMMAL

CAITIE MCANENEY

PowerKiDS press
New York

Published in 2020 by The Rosen Publishing Group, Inc.
29 East 21st Street, New York, NY 10010

First Edition

Editor: Theresa Emminizer
Book Design: Reann Nye

Photo Credits: Series Art (frame) HiSunnySky/Shutterstock.com; Series Art (Banners) Roberto Castillo/Shutterstock.com; Series Art (background) Wilqkuku/Shutterstock.com; Cover Donovan van Staden/Shutterstock.com; p. 5 Anup Shah/Corbis Documentary/ Getty Images Plus/Getty Images; p. 7 Andrzej Kubik/Shutterstock.com; p. 9 Four Oaks/Shutterstock.com; p. 11 Paul Hampton/ Shutterstock.com; p. 13 Frank Lukasseck/ Corbis Documentary / Getty Images Plus/Getty Images; pp. 15, 19 Villiers Steyn/ Shutterstock.com; p. 17 kavram/Shutterstock.com; p. 21 Maciej Czekajewski/Shutterstock.com; p. 22 Grobler du Preez/ Shutterstock.com.

Cataloging-in-Publication Data

Names: McAneney, Caitie.
Title: African elephant: the largest land mammal / Caitie McAneney.
Description: New York : PowerKids Press, 2020. | Series: Animal record breakers | Includes glossary and index.
Identifiers: ISBN 9781725308589 (pbk.) | ISBN 9781725308602 (library bound) | ISBN 9781725308596 (6 pack)
Subjects: LCSH: African elephant–Juvenile literature.
Classification: LCC QL737.P98 M39 2020 | DDC 599.67'4–dc23

Manufactured in the United States of America

CPSIA Compliance Information: Batch #CWPK20. For Further Information contact Rosen Publishing, New York, New York at 1-800-237-9932.

CONTENTS

LARGEST IN THE LAND........................4
THE ELEPHANT FAMILY 6
BIG BODIES 8
SPECIAL SKILLS...........................10
HUNGRY, HUNGRY ELEPHANTS 12
SPEAK LIKE AN ELEPHANT 14
ELEPHANTS ON THE MAP 16
AN ELEPHANT'S LIFE 18
FACING THREATS 20
SAVE THE ELEPHANT!.................... 22
GLOSSARY 23
INDEX................................. 24
WEBSITES.............................. 24

LARGEST IN THE LAND

African elephants are the largest **mammals** that walk on Earth. They can grow up to 13 feet (4 m) tall from their feet to their shoulders and can weigh up to 7 tons (6.4 mt).

African elephants have more than just size on their side. They also have amazing **senses** and skills for survival. From sensing small movements in the ground to living closely in herds, African elephants are some of the most interesting animals in the world.

African elephant babies stay close to their herd for safety.

THE ELEPHANT FAMILY

Elephants are pachyderms. That's a kind of mammal with very strong, thick skin. Pachyderms include elephants and rhinoceroses. Elephant skin is about an inch (2.5 cm) thick in places.

There are two species, or kinds, of elephants—Asian elephants and African elephants. Asian elephants are smaller than African elephants. African elephants are broken into two smaller groups—forest elephants and savanna elephants. Savanna elephants are even bigger than forest elephants. Their tusks (long, pointed teeth) curve up. Forest elephants have straighter tusks.

ANIMAL ACTION

Forest elephants have **adapted** to their **habitats**. They can be found in the forests of the Congo Basin.

The savanna is a grassy area of land with few trees and bushes. About half of Africa is a savanna habitat.

BIG BODIES

African elephants' bodies have adapted to fit their habitat. Their saggy skin and big ears help to keep them cool. They also use their long, noselike parts—called trunks—to spray their bodies with water and dust.

Elephant trunks are great tools, with around 100,000 **muscles**. Elephants smell, drink, and breathe through their trunks. They also use their trunks to **communicate** with each other and to grab and hold objects. Elephants use their long tusks to dig for water and food.

ELEPHANT ANATOMY

Anatomy is the study of the body of a living creature.

SPECIAL SKILLS

African elephants depend on their strong family bonds to survive. While male elephants often walk alone, females and young elephants form herds to take care of each other. They can even recognize one another.

Elephants have super senses of hearing, smell, and touch. They can hear calls from other elephants almost a mile (1.6 km) away. They can smell water up to 12 miles (19.3 km) away. Their trunks and feet can feel tiny **vibrations** in the ground that help them sense things moving.

ANIMAL ACTION

Elephants have such close bonds that they mourn, or show sadness about, their dead. They are known to visit the remains of dead members of their herd.

Elephants "hear" the earth through vibrations. They can "hear" calls, animals coming closer, and even faraway earthquakes.

HUNGRY, HUNGRY ELEPHANTS

A big body means a big appetite, or need for food. Elephants are herbivores, or animals that eat only plants. And they need a lot of plant matter to live and grow. In fact, one adult elephant can eat up to 300 pounds (136 kg) of food in a single day!

Elephants eat small plants, twigs, tree bark, fruit, grass, and even soil. They often use their tusks to strip bark off trees or to dig for roots to eat.

ANIMAL ACTION

Elephants can drink up to 40 gallons (151.4 l) of water every day. They can go for up to four days without water, but they will use their trunks to dig for it if they need to.

Elephants spend much of their time walking from place to place, looking for food and water.

SPEAK LIKE AN ELEPHANT

As herd animals, communication is very important to elephants. When they greet one another, they put their trunks in each other's mouths, almost like a handshake! They also do this to say "sorry." A happy elephant will bounce around and swing its trunk.

When an elephant wants to tell another elephant to "back off," it will charge at the elephant, stop, and stomp. That says it means business. When nervous, elephants might suck on the tip of their trunk, like a baby sucking its thumb.

When an elephant is unhappy, it will put its ears out and shake its big, dusty head.

ELEPHANTS ON THE MAP

Where in the world can you find an African elephant? Only in Africa, of course! Forest elephants live in forests of western and central Africa, close to the **equator**. Areas along the equator are some of the hottest places on Earth. Savanna elephants live on the hot, grassy plains of eastern and southern Africa.

Other savanna animals include zebras, giraffes, wildebeests, and warthogs. Predators include lions, cheetahs, and hyenas. Adult African elephants are **protected** from predators by their size and thick skin.

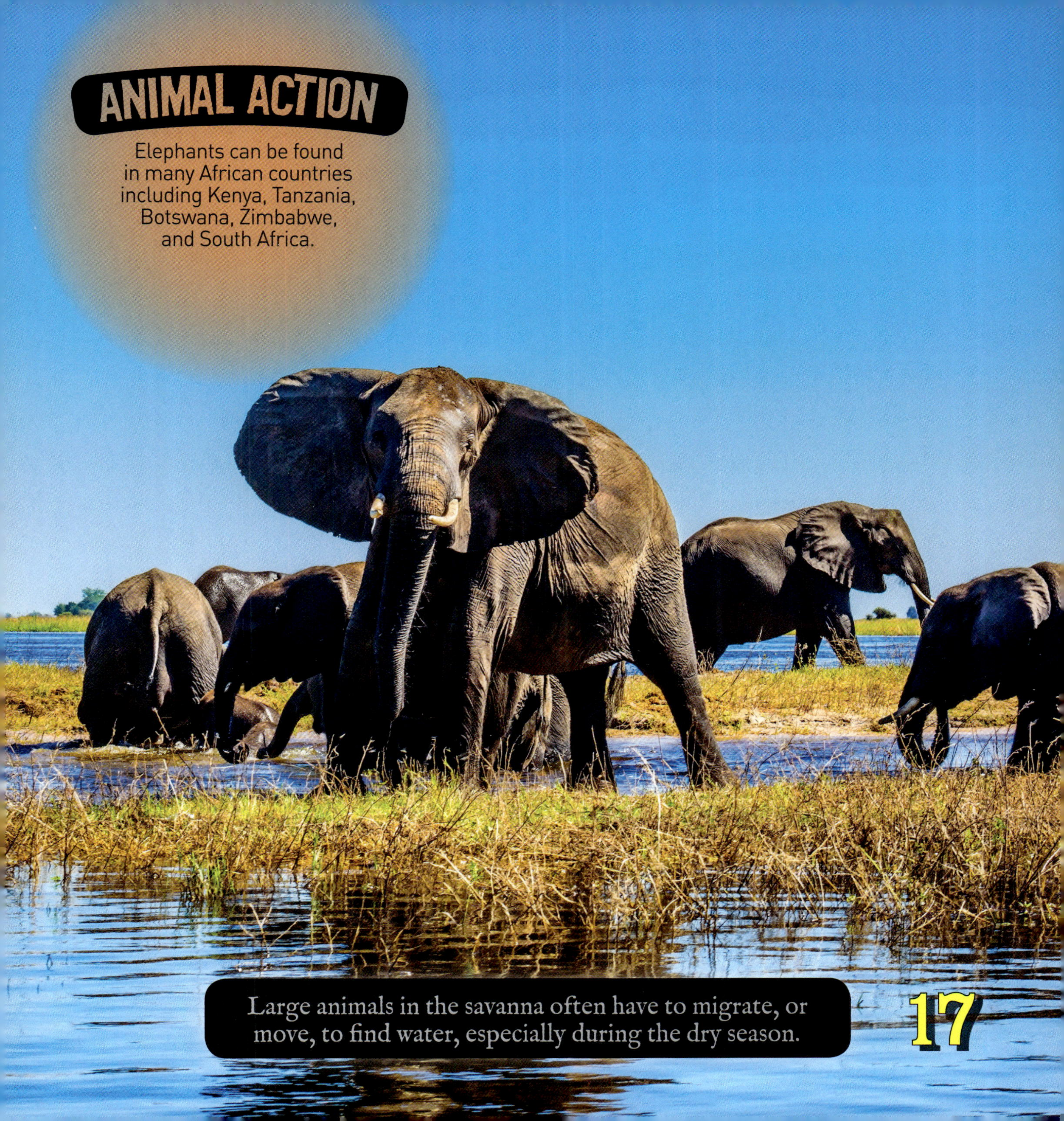

ANIMAL ACTION

Elephants can be found in many African countries including Kenya, Tanzania, Botswana, Zimbabwe, and South Africa.

Large animals in the savanna often have to migrate, or move, to find water, especially during the dry season.

AN ELEPHANT'S LIFE

Elephant babies, or calves, make a big entrance into the world. They grow inside their mother for 22 months. At birth they are about 3 feet (0.9 m) tall and weigh about 200 pounds (90.7 kg). Baby elephants are protected by their herd and depend on their mothers for milk.

Female elephants have babies when they're around 25 to 45 years old. They only give birth to one calf at a time. African elephants live to be about 70 years old in the wild.

ANIMAL ACTION

Elephants have the longest gestation of any mammal in the world. Gestation is the time a mother carries a baby in her body.

Baby elephants drink their mother's milk for up to 6 years. During the first year of life, they gain 2 to 3 pounds (0.9 kg to 1.36 kg) a day just on milk.

FACING THREATS

Elephants have few natural predators, but face serious **threats** from humans. They are listed as vulnerable, meaning they're in danger of dying out if things don't get better. While their population, or number, used to be up to 5 million, it is now around 415,000.

African elephants have lost 50 percent of their natural habitat from farms, businesses, and homes being built. When elephants enter farms, farmers sometimes kill them in anger. Also, elephants are poached, or illegally hunted, for their tusks, skin, and meat.

Poachers sell elephant tusks because they are rare, or uncommon. They are made into ivory, which is used to make jewelry and other items.

SAVE THE ELEPHANT!

African elephants are amazing animals. They live in some of the hottest places on Earth and survive using special adaptations. African elephants help keep habitats healthy by spreading seeds to grow trees and by shaping the land as they move across it.

As the greatest threat to their survival, humans must make an effort to protect African elephants and their habitats. Together, we can make sure that African Elephants continue to wander the forests and savannas of Africa for many years to come.

GLOSSARY

adapt: To change in order to live better in a certain environment.

communicate: To share ideas and feelings through sounds and motions.

equator: The imaginary east-west line that circles around Earth midway between the North and South poles.

habitat: The natural home for plants, animals, and other living things.

mammal: Any warm-blooded animal whose babies drink milk and whose body has hair or fur.

muscle: A part of the body that produces motion.

protect: To keep safe.

senses: Taste, smell, touch, hearing, and sight.

threat: Someone or something that could cause harm.

vibration: A small, quick movement.

INDEX

A
adapted, 8
Asian elephants, 6

C
calves, 18
communication, 8, 14

F
food, 12
forest elephants, 6, 16

H
herds, 10, 14, 18

P
pachyderm, 6
poaching, 20
predators, 16, 20

S
savanna elephants, 6, 16

T
trunks, 8, 14
tusks, 6, 8, 12, 20

WEBSITES

Due to the changing nature of Internet links, PowerKids Press has developed an online list of websites related to the subject of this book. This site is updated regularly. Please use this link to access the list: www.powerkidslinks.com/arb/elephant